Manatees for Kids

by Patricia Corrigan
illustrated by John F. McGee

NORTHWORD
NORTHWORD PRESS, INC.
Minocqua, Wisconsin

WILDLIFE *For Kids* SERIES

DEDICATION

To Edward Murphey Coffield
(a fellow manatee lover and part-time muse)
and all kids who love manatees

© Patricia Corrigan, 1996
Photography © 1996 by: Doug Perrine/Innnerspace Visions, Cover, 28-29; Kennan Ward, 3; Daniel J. Cox/Natural Exposures, 6, 18-19, 36-37, 42-43; Jeff Foott, 7, 10, 15, 16, 30-31, Back Cover; Art Wolfe, 12; Brandon Cole, 23, 24, 34, 41, 46.

NorthWord Press, Inc.
P.O. Box 1360
Minocqua, WI 54548

Illustrations by John F. McGee
Book design by Lisa Moore

The **NATIONAL WILDLIFE FEDERATION®** is the nation's largest, non-profit, conservation education organization. Since 1936, NWF has educated people from all walks of life to protect nature, wildlife and the world we all share.

Library of Congress Cataloging-in-Publication Data

Corrigan, Patricia.
    Manatees for kids / by Patricia Corrigan.
        p.   cm.
        Summary: Facts about manatees presented through the investigations of an inquisitive nearly eleven-year-old girl.
        ISBN 1-55971-539-1 (sc)
        1. Manatees--Juvenile literature. [1. Manatees.] I. Title.
QL737.S63C68 1996
599.5'5–dc20   95-32806

Printed in Malaysia

Manatees for Kids

by Patricia Corrigan
illustrated by John F. McGee

All of the photographs in this book are of Florida manatees

All my life, I've wanted to be a mermaid . . . those beautiful creatures that are half woman and half fish.

Imagine living in the sea, swimming every day in the sun, going for rides on the backs of dolphins, and attending tea parties with colorful tropical fish.

My big brother thinks I'm silly.

Edward says there is no such thing as a mermaid. I'm not convinced. If there are no mermaids, how come everybody knows about them?

My name is Amanda. I'm nearly 11. I have long curly brown hair, and I know how to swim, so I'm already almost a mermaid.

My brother says his science teacher told his class that the legend of the mermaid is based on a marine mammal called a manatee. (That's pronounced just like it looks: MAN-AH-TEE.)

What is a manatee?

I didn't know, until Edward showed me a picture.
Now I'm very confused.

Manatees don't have long, beautiful hair. They don't
have elegant, fish-like tails. They don't look like they go
to underwater tea parties, either.

The manatee in the picture I saw looks sort of like a
walrus. It has squinty little eyes, and whiskers all over
its broad, flat face and chin. The manatee's big, rum-
pled body is brownish-gray—or is it grayish-brown? It
has two short flippers and a broad, flat tail, sort of like
a beaver's.

"This is supposed to be a mermaid?" I said.

Edward grinned.

"Not exactly. My teacher said that sailors who had been at sea for a long time mistook manatees for beautiful women who live underwater.

"The legend is that these mermaids sat on rocks and sang haunting, beautiful songs. When sailors moved in for a closer look, their ships were wrecked on the rocks, and the sailors drowned."

"Are manatees mean?" I asked.

"I don't think so," Edward said. "I do know they don't eat sailors. Manatees are vegetarians. They eat plants."

The teacher told his class that manatees are gentle, slow-moving creatures. Most manatees grow to 10 or 11 feet long and weigh about 1,200 pounds. Some really big manatees may weigh as much as 3,000 pounds. Usually, females are bigger than males.

"Oh, I remember one more thing," Edward said. "Some people call manatees 'sea cows.'"

I decided to find out for myself about these manatees. Edward let me borrow his science book. I learned some important facts.

For instance: There are several different species of manatees. The one that lives in the United States is a type of West Indian manatee commonly called the Florida manatee.

Just as Edward said, manatees are gentle, and they move slowly through the water. They cannot move their heads from side to side, so manatees turn their entire bodies to look in another direction. Most manatees spend their time in shallow rivers and canals, or along coastal areas. There, they eat sea grasses and plants that grow on the bottom of the river and along the shore.

Manatees chew about two times every second—
a scientist timed them. They spend much of their time
eating, and their teeth wear out quickly. As worn-out
teeth fall out, new teeth growing at the back of the
animal's jaw quickly replace them.

Edward's book showed a picture of a manatee eating a flower called a water hyacinth (HI-AH-SINTH). The manatee was holding the stem with its flippers. I could see three fingernails on each flipper! The fingernails look just like an elephant's toenails. Unlike my mom's fingernails, the manatee's nails were not painted bright red. Maybe the fingernails were left over from when the manatee was a land animal, millions of years ago.

Manatees breathe air, as we do, so they must float to the water's surface every three to five minutes. There, they stick their noses out and take a breath. When they are under water, a special flap closes over their noses. Manatees also have special protective lids for their eyes.

Manatees' ears are just tiny openings, not far from their eyes. Still, they hear well. Manatees make several different sounds: chirps, whistles and squeaks. The sounds help the animals keep track of one another in murky water. Mother manatees (called cows) and their babies (called calves) often squeak and chirp to one another. The animals make different kinds of chirps and squeaks to welcome an arriving manatee or to signal fear. Some scientists think that manatees can make, and also hear, very low sounds.

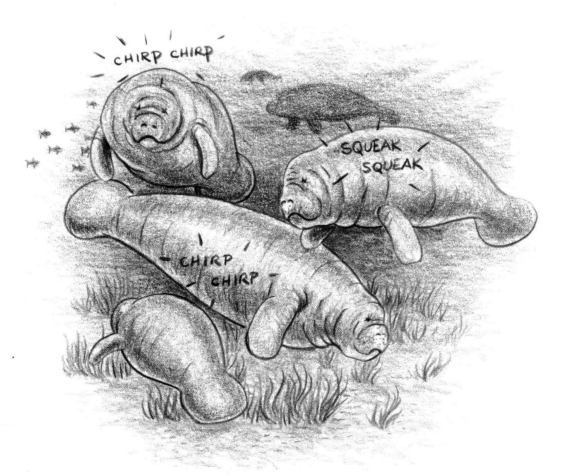

Manatees spend their days mostly eating, swimming, resting and playing. Sometimes, manatees snuggle against one another, like cats that are friends. They rub noses, too. Sometimes, they hug one another with their flippers.

Manatees usually swim slowly, twisting and turning gracefully in the water. Manatees don't seem to mind swimming completely upside down or even sideways! Sometimes, they appear to play "Follow the Leader," forming a line and following one particular manatee. During the game, they all swim in the same direction, breathe at the same time, and dive together–imitating the lead manatee.

What a lovely life!

Even though they swim slowly, manatees can travel great distances. One manatee swam about 500 miles. Scientists know of another that traveled more than 140 miles in just four days.

Many manatees spend the winter in Florida, where they find warm spring waters to wait out the winter.

Another type of West Indian manatee is the Antillean (ANN-TILL-YAN) manatee. There are two other species: the West African manatee and Amazonian (AM-AH-ZONE-EE-ANN) manatee.

Manatees have lived on Earth a long time. Fossils prove that a creature distantly related to manatees lived about 35 million years ago. An animal much like manatees that we know lived 15 million years ago. Today's manatees all are distant cousins to elephants!

Another animal related to manatees is the dugong (DOO-GONG). Dugongs live far away, off Australia in the Pacific Ocean and in the Indian Ocean. Dugongs grow to only about half the size of manatees. Their bodies are smoother. Dugongs' tails are not paddle-shaped, like manatees' tails, but look like whales' tails.

Guess what? A common name for the dugong is "mermaid!"

Maybe it was the dugong that those sailors of long ago mistook for mermaids.

Dugongs don't have long, beautiful hair. But I think you might be likelier to mistake a dugong for a woman singing in the water than a bulky, wrinkled manatee. Of course, neither manatees nor dugongs sing. My mom said maybe the sailors were hearing humpback whales through the wooden hulls of the boats. Humpbacks do sing beautiful songs.

A long time ago, in the 1700s, explorers shipwrecked on an island in the Bering Sea found a creature in the water that they had never seen before.

A German scientist named G. W. Steller was among those shipwrecked on the island. He kept a notebook. In it, he carefully described the animals, which he named Steller's sea cows.

The sea cows were three times bigger than the Florida manatee. Some of them were more than 30 feet long and weighed several tons. The Steller's sea cow looked half like a manatee with its wrinkled skin, and half like a dugong with its whale-like tail.

The Steller's sea cows were dark brown, with some white on their bodies. They had no teeth, but they didn't need any. The sea cows ate different kinds of seaweed.

When the explorers first were shipwrecked in 1741, there were between 1,500 and 2,000 sea cows in the Bering Strait. By 1768, just 27 years later, every sea cow had been killed for its meat.

Now they are extinct.

Some islanders in the Pacific Ocean believe that manatees are evil spirits. Only a few people on the islands know the secret words that allow them to hunt manatees without coming under the spell of the evil spirit. One Indian tribe in South America says that manatees are bewitched human beings who live in cities at the bottom of the river.

The Florida manatee is an endangered species, and may become extinct.

The manatee has no natural enemies. Even alligators stay away from them, probably because manatees are so big. But Florida is a popular state, and many, many people live right on the canals and rivers that are natural habitats for the manatees. When people move in and build boat docks, the sea grasses and water plants disappear.

Every year, some manatees die from injuries they get when boats run over them. Some die from pollution, from the poisons that find their way into the water. Some die from eating plastic litter that people throw in the water. Some winters, manatees can't find a warm place to live, and they die from the cold.

To protect the manatees, Florida has passed laws to keep people from running their boats too fast. Also, no one is allowed to hunt or kill manatees. The state is working to find ways so that people and manatees can live in harmony.

No one knows exactly how many Florida manatees are alive today, but scientists think there only are about 1,800. That's not very many.

Manatees can give birth only every two to five years, to one calf at a time. The calves are about four feet long when they are born, and can weigh as much as 65 pounds. A calf nurses under its mother's "armpit" for up to two years, taking in rich milk from its mother while underwater. But calves are born with teeth, too, and they will nibble on plants just a few weeks after birth.

I began to worry that manatees might disappear from the Earth before I got to meet one. I told Edward and together we asked our parents to take us to Florida.

My dad and I wrote for some information on the different places to see manatees, and then we made the trip.

My family traveled to Homosassa (HO-MO-SASS-A) Springs, in Citrus County on the northwest coast of Florida. The first morning, we went for a boat ride on the Homosassa River. We rode along, looking at the many birds that live on the water, when suddenly the captain said he saw several manatees up ahead.

I stared and stared at the water. Just when I was about to give up, a little nose popped up out of the river, not too far from the boat. Then it disappeared.

"It's a manatee! My first manatee!" I said.

Even Edward thought it was exciting. The water was a little muddy, but I could see the outline of the manatee's body in the river. The captain said three adult manatees and one calf were nearby. He suggested that my family visit a wildlife park that afternoon for a closer look at manatees.

Ten manatees–eight adult females and two male calves–live at the Homosassa Springs Wildlife Park, in a part of the river that has been blocked off to protect them. The park is one of several places in Florida that cares for injured manatees.

Anyone who sees a sick or injured manatee is encouraged to call a special number to report it. Wildlife officials immediately go to the area where the animal was seen, and rescue it with special slings and nets. Then, they carefully transport the manatee to the closest place that cares for the animals.

There, workers medicate open cuts made by boat propellers. They prepare formula for orphaned calves. They feed starving animals. They remove any fishing line wrapped around a flipper or the tail.

They do whatever they have to do to save the manatee. If possible, the animals are released back into the wild when their injuries have healed.

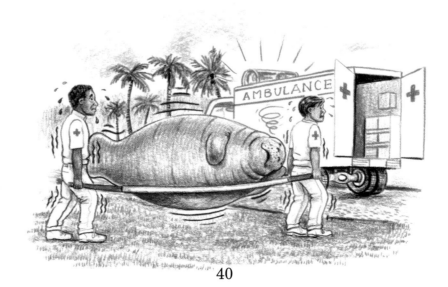

We went out onto an observation platform at the park. When I looked down into the clear water, I saw a mother manatee nursing her calf! Another manatee drifted slowly by. I could see the scars on her back, where boat propellers had cut her. Then, she flicked her big tail and zipped away.

Downstairs at the observatory, below the water's surface, I peered out a big window at hundreds of fascinating-looking fish. I picked up a telephone connected to an underwater microphone. Suddenly I heard a loud squeaking sound in the phone.

Edward motioned for me to turn toward the window. A huge manatee was passing by, right through all those fish!

The manatee was floating gracefully, completely upside down. She looked like she had a little grin on her face. I stared right into her eyes! When the manatee drifted away, we all went upstairs and walked to the other side of the river bank, where we took seats for a short program.

A wildlife specialist dressed in waterproof pants waded into the water. All 10 manatees crowded around him. He held a bright yellow bucket full of biscuits made from nutritional grains–a snack he said the manatees like.

As he talked to us about manatees, suddenly, one really big manatee swam in front of the wildlife specialist. I think it was the same manatee that grinned at me earlier.

She stuck her whole head up out of the water!

"Would you like a biscuit?" the man asked the manatee.

She nodded her head up and down, splashing water everywhere. She didn't stop until he put a biscuit in her mouth!

"We call this one Amanda," he said.

Amanda–that's my name!

I came all this way to meet a manatee, and we have the very same name.

Manatees may not be beautiful creatures that are half woman and half fish. They may not live in the sea, or swim every day in the sun. They may not go for rides on the backs of dolphins, or attend tea parties with colorful tropical fish.

But now I believe that real manatees are every bit as wonderful as mythical mermaids.

Especially the one named Amanda.